Bernd Wehren

Bildimpulse zum kreativen Schreiben im Englischunterricht

Differenzierte Arbeitsblätter für die Klassen 5–7

HOTEL

sun

sand

ice cream

couple

beach

sunglasses

The girl is building a castle in the sand.
The boy is eating ice cream.
There are a lot of people on the beach.

Verlag an der Ruhr

Impressum

Titel
Bildimpulse zum kreativen Schreiben im Englischunterricht
Differenzierte Arbeitsblätter für die Klassen 5–7

Autor
Bernd Wehren

Umschlagmotive
Strand: Bettina Weyland
Stift/Figuren mit Stiften: © Bibadash – Shutterstock.com

Illustrationen
Bettina Weyland

Druck
Heenemann GmbH & Co. KG, Berlin, DE

Verlag an der Ruhr
Mülheim an der Ruhr
www.verlagruhr.de

Geeignet für die Klassen 5–7

ISBN 978-3-8346-6494-5

Inhaltsverzeichnis

Vorwort

Kreatives Schreiben bietet für den **handlungsorientierten fremdsprachlichen Unterricht** viele Vorteile. Wie die Sprachlernforschung gezeigt hat, können Schüler*innen[1] eine Sprache vor allem dann gut lernen, wenn sie sich beim Üben und Experimentieren affektiv mit einem Thema auseinandersetzen und ihre Erfahrungen und Fantasie einbringen können. Kreatives Schreiben aktiviert das **Vorstellungsvermögen** und motiviert die Lernenden, ihre schriftlichen Ausdrucksfähigkeiten zu erproben sowie ihren Wortschatz zu erweitern, um eine für sie **bedeutsame Geschichte** zu erzählen. Im Fokus steht die **Freude am Schreiben**, was eine angenehme Lernatmosphäre schafft und sich positiv auf die langfristige Entwicklung der Kommunikationsfähigkeiten auswirkt.

In den **Kernlehrplänen für das Fach Englisch** ist das kreative Schreiben daher aus gutem Grund bereits in den Klassen 5 und 6 fest verankert. So sollen Lernende z. B. in Thüringen „unter Verwendung elementarer sprachlicher Mittel [...] Erlebtes, Erdachtes und nach Impulsen erzählen"[2] oder in Bayern „mithilfe inhaltlicher Vorgaben kurze Texte [...] zu Themen aus ihrer persönlichen Erfahrungswelt"[3] verfassen können. Hier setzt das vorliegende Heft an.

Bildimpulse zum kreativen Schreiben

Mithilfe der Bildimpulse und zugehörigen Arbeitsaufträge fördern Sie die **Schreibkompetenz** Ihrer Schüler*innen. Die Themen der 15 **Erzähl- und Schreibanlässe** basieren auf den Kernlehrplänen Englisch für die Klassen 5 und 6 und passen daher zu vielen Lehrbuchtexten und zur Lebenswelt der Lernenden. Die Bilder können dabei sowohl Ausgangspunkt als auch Endpunkt des Geschehens sein; der Kreativität Ihrer Schüler*innen sind keine Grenzen gesetzt.

Didaktisch-methodische Hinweise

Die Arbeitsblätter sind 2-fach differenziert und enthalten jeweils aufeinander aufbauende Aufgaben, die den **Schreibprozess vorentlasten**. Sie bieten Struktur, lassen den Lernenden aber auch den Freiraum, ihre eigenen Ideen einzubringen.

Sowohl in der leichteren als auch in der schwierigeren Ausführung werden die Schüler*innen zunächst animiert, das **Bild genau zu betrachten**, indem sie **sinnvolle Ergänzungen** vornehmen. Sie können beispielsweise fehlende Elemente ergänzen, zusätzliche Charaktere oder Gegenstände einfügen, Sprechblasen malen und etwas hineinschreiben. So gestalten die Schüler*innen ihre Geschichte von vornherein selbst mit.

Den differenzierten Arbeitsblättern sind jeweils Kopiervorlagen vorangestellt, die ein **vollständiges Bild** zeigen und z. B. bei der Wortschatzarbeit oder als Vorlage zum Üben einer Bildbeschreibung eingesetzt werden können.

a) einfacher:
Die einfachere Variante erkennen Sie an einem Punkt. Die Schüler*innen malen das Wimmelbild weiter und wählen aus zwei Vorschlägen eine zur dargestellten Situation passende Überschrift aus. Anschließend aktivieren sie ihren Wortschatz, indem sie vorgegebene Wörter

[1] Der Verlag an der Ruhr legt großen Wert auf eine geschlechtergerechte und inklusive Sprache. Daher nutzen wir neutrale Formulierungen oder das Gendersternchen, um alle Menschen unabhängig von Geschlecht oder Geschlechtsidentität einzuschließen. In Texten für Schüler*innen finden sich aus didaktischen Gründen neutrale Begriffe bzw. Doppelformen.

[2] Thüringer Ministerium für Bildung, Wissenschaft und Kultur (2011): Lehrplan für den Erwerb des Hauptschul- und des Realschulabschlusses. Englisch, S. 24.

[3] Staatsinstitut für Schulqualität und Bildungsforschung München (2023): Lehrplan für die bayerische Realschule, S. 531.

Vorwort

den entsprechenden Elementen im Bild zuordnen. Hierbei sind nicht nur Nomen, sondern auch Verben enthalten. Dann vervollständigen die Lernenden vorstrukturierte Sätze, indem sie beschreiben, was sie im Bild sehen und was die Personen tun. Optional können nun noch drei bis fünf weitere Sätze geschrieben werden.
*Tipp: Sie können den Schüler*innen die Aufgabe stellen, weitere Wörter zu notieren, nachdem sie das Bild ergänzt haben.*

b) schwieriger:
Die schwierigere Variante erkennen Sie an zwei Punkten. Die Schüler*innen malen das Wimmelbild weiter und schreiben eine eigene, thematisch passende Überschrift auf. Sie notieren passende Wörter zum Bild und aktivieren so ihren Wortschatz. Hierbei sind geeignete Nomen sowie oft auch passende Adjektive und Verben als Beispiele angeführt, die den Schüler*innen als Inspiration dienen können. Anschließend schreiben die Lernenden eine Geschichte zu dem Bild und benutzen dabei die zuvor notierten Vokabeln.
Tipp: Zur weiteren Differenzierung können die Hilfekarten beim Planen, Schreiben und Korrigieren der Geschichte eingesetzt werden.

Zum Einsatz der Materialien

a) Arbeitsblätter (S. 6–50):
Sie können entweder zuerst die einfacheren Arbeitsblätter, dann die schwierigeren Arbeitsblätter bearbeiten lassen oder Sie bieten stets neben dem jeweils leichteren Arbeitsblatt auch das dazugehörige schwierigere Arbeitsblatt für schreibstarke Schüler*innen an. Selbstverständlich können Sie auch eine gezielte Auswahl der Arbeitsblätter für die Schüler*innen treffen.

b) Hilfekarten (S. 51–55):
Die Hilfekarten unterstützen beim

Planen,

Schreiben  und

Überarbeiten von Texten. Sie können laminiert im Klassenraum bereitliegen oder für jedes Kind kopiert werden, um auch bei der Bearbeitung der Arbeitsblätter z. B. als Hausaufgabe griffbereit zu sein. Im Sinne der funktionalen Einsprachigkeit sind diese Karten auf Deutsch verfasst.

c) Selbsteinschätzungsbogen (S. 56):
Damit Ihre Schüler*innen den Schreibprozess reflektieren können, finden Sie am Ende des Hefts einen Selbsteinschätzungsbogen.

d) Download:
Sie finden alle Bildimpulse sowohl in der vollständigen Variante als auch in der Variante mit Lücken im Download, sodass Sie die Bilder bequem über einen Beamer bzw. eine digitale Tafel im Plenum präsentieren können.

Ihr persönlicher Zugang:
Alle im Download enthaltenen Dateien können Sie unter folgendem Link oder über das Einscannen des QR-Codes herunterladen:

https://cloud.verlagruhr.de/lerninhalt/8O9qQhODRBwL/

Passwort: Bildimpulse-Englisch!
Sollten der Link und der QR-Code ihre Gültigkeit verlieren, wenden Sie sich bitte an digitaleslernen@verlagruhr.de

Home

Home

1. **What is missing?** Complete the picture below.
2. **What is the situation?** Pick a title.
   - ▢ Relaxing at home
   - ▢ Tidying up together
3. **What can you see in the picture?** Connect the words with the picture.

window • garden • stairs • living room • bathroom • kitchen • roof • to put away

door • shower • wall • to clean • oven • table • chair • cupboard • tree • clothes

4. **What is happening?** Complete the sentences.

Early in the morning, the family ....

Today, they ....

Everyone in the family ....

Later, ...

Write 3–5 more sentences on the back of this worksheet.

Home

1. **What is missing?** Complete the picture below.
2. **What is the situation?** Give the picture a title.

....

3. **What can you see in the picture?** Write down words.

   house – to tidy up – garden –

4. **What is happening?** Write your story on a piece of paper.

Give each person a name and say where they are.
Describe what everyone is doing.
Think about what will happen next.

Party

Party

1. **What is missing?** Complete the picture below.
2. **What is the situation?** Pick a title.
   - ☐ The birthday party
   - ☐ The pyjama party
3. **What can you see in the picture?** Connect the words with the picture.

   box • cake • present • to say • candle • balloons • table • crown

to smile • swimming pool • chair • glass • plate • to think • party • ball

4. **What is happening?** Complete the sentences.

   Today's a special day because ....

   In the afternoon, ...

   The kids ....

   The birthday boy ....

Write 3–5 more sentences on the back of this worksheet.

Party

1. **What is missing?** Complete the picture below.
2. **What is the situation?** Give the picture a title.

....

3. **What can you see in the picture?** Write down words.

   cake – happy – to think – ....

   ....

   ....

   ....

4. **What is happening?** Write your story on a piece of paper.

Give each person a name and say where they are.
Describe what everyone is doing.
Think about what will happen next.

Letter

Letter

1. **What is missing?** Complete the picture below.
2. **What is the situation?** Pick a title.
   - ▢ Going to school
   - ▢ Writing a letter
3. **What can you see in the picture?** Connect the words with the picture.

mailman • desk • to think • hat • letter • elephant • bookshelf • t-shirt

socks • bag • pencil • mailbox • paper • ball • toy car • rucksack

4. **What is happening?** Complete the sentences.

.... is sitting on his desk and ....

He is writing a letter because ....

He is thinking about ....

Outside the window, ...

Write 3–5 more sentences on the back of this worksheet.

Letter

1. **What is missing?** Complete the picture below.
2. **What is the situation?** Give the picture a title.

....

3. **What can you see in the picture?** Write down words.

mailman – to think – bookshelf – ....

....

....

....

4. **What is happening?** Write your story on a piece of paper.

Give each person a name and say where they are.
Describe what everyone is doing.
Think about what will happen next.

Stories about friends & family

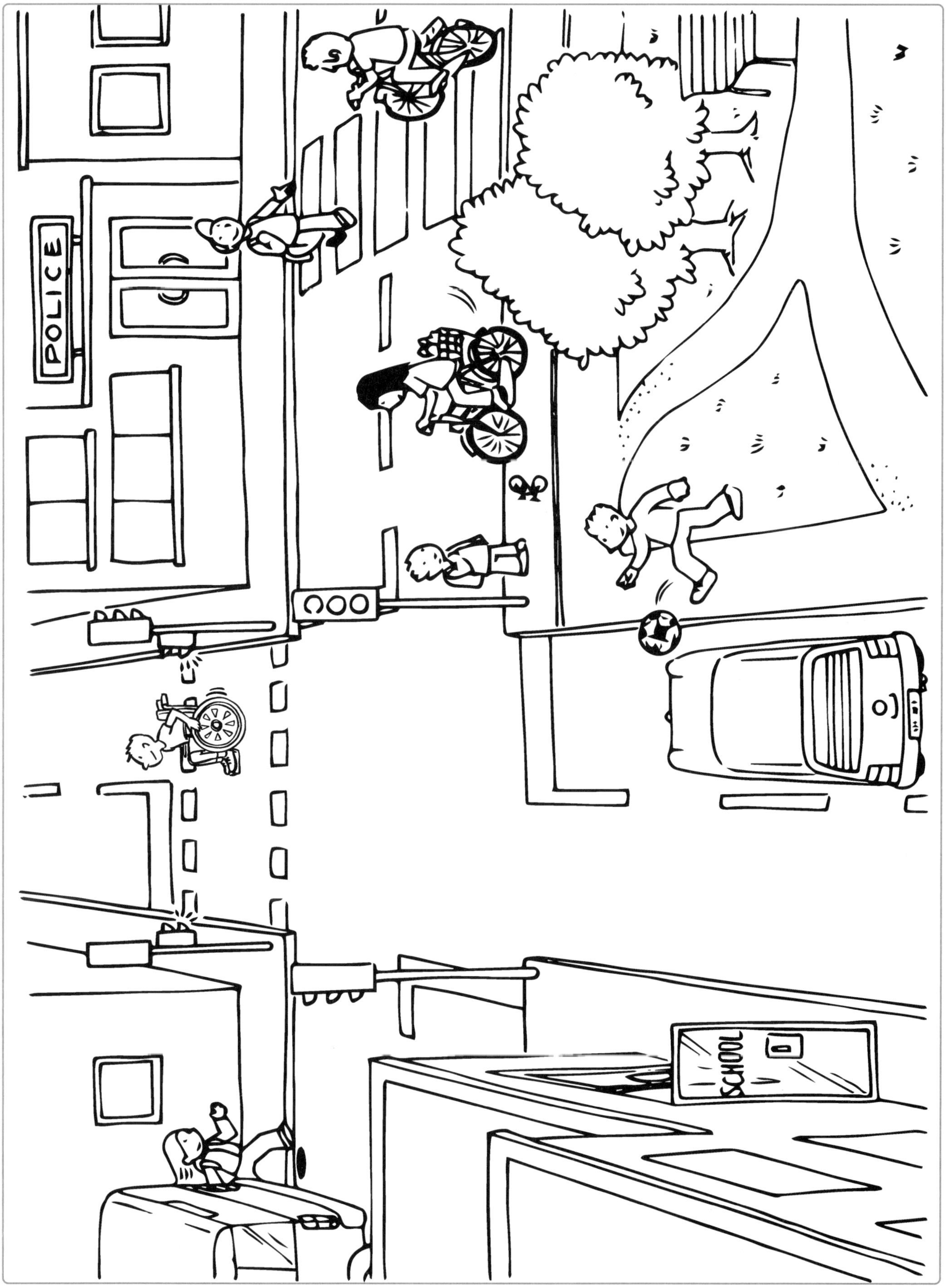

City

1. **What is missing?** Complete the picture below.
2. **What is the situation?** Pick a title.
   - ▢ A day in the city
   - ▢ A day at the beach
3. **What can you see in the picture?** Connect the words with the picture.

traffic light • street • house • bus • bike • to cross the street • window

door • car • park • to kick • grass • hat • bench • tree

4. **What is happening?** Complete the sentences.

In the city, ...

A boy ....

Next, ...

A girl ....

Write 3–5 more sentences on the back of this worksheet.

City

1. **What is missing?** Complete the picture below.
2. **What is the situation?** Give the picture a title.

....

3. **What can you see in the picture?** Write down words.

traffic light – to kick – to cross the street – ....

....

....

....

4. **What is happening?** Write your story on a piece of paper.

Give each person a name and say where they are.
Describe what everyone is doing.
Think about what will happen next.

Skatepark

Stories about sports & activities

Skatepark

1. **What is missing?** Complete the picture below.
2. **What is the situation?** Pick a title.
   - ☐ At the skate park
   - ☐ At school
3. **What can you see in the picture?** Connect the words with the picture.

helmet • to skate • tree • to walk • kiosk • to jump • bush • inline skates

cap • scooter • halfpipe • skateboard • knee protector • sneakers • drink • to buy

4. **What is happening?** Complete the sentences.

On a sunny day, ...

There, they ....

.... can do the best tricks.

At the kiosk, ...

Write 3–5 more sentences on the back of this worksheet.

Skatepark

1. **What is missing?** Complete the picture below.
2. **What is the situation?** Give the picture a title.

....

3. **What can you see in the picture?** Write down words.

helmet – to skate – to buy – ....

....

....

....

4. **What is happening?** Write your story on a piece of paper.

Give each person a name and say where they are.
Describe what everyone is doing.
Think about what will happen next.

Pool

Stories about sports & activities

Pool

1. **What is missing?** Complete the picture below.
2. **What is the situation?** Pick a title.
   - ▢ A day on the beach
   - ▢ A day at the pool
3. **What can you see in the picture?** Connect the words with the picture.

t-shirt • water • legs • ladder • swim shorts • to jump • to run • window

lifeguard • flip-flops • feet • to throw • poster • bikini • ball • to smile

4. **What is happening?** Complete the sentences.

Every Sunday, the kids ....

They ....

One of the boys ....,

but..

Write 3–5 more sentences on the back of this worksheet.

Pool

1. **What is missing?** Complete the picture below.
2. **What is the situation?** Give the picture a title.

....

3. **What can you see in the picture?** Write down words.

ball – to jump – swim shorts – ....

....

....

....

4. **What is happening?** Write your story on a piece of paper.

Give each person a name and say where they are.
Describe what everyone is doing.
Think about what will happen next.

Sports

Stories about sports & activities

Sports

1. **What is missing?** Complete the picture below.
2. **What is the situation?** Pick a title.
   - ☐ Having fun in PE class
   - ☐ Having fun in chemistry class
3. **What can you see in the picture?** Connect the words with the picture.

   t-shirt • ladder • to dance • to kick • badminton • to play • ball • rope

to climb • tennis shoes • radio • to smile • shorts • to do a handstand

4. **What is happening?** Complete the sentences.

In PE class, ...

Some pupils ....

A girl ....

A boy ....

Write 3–5 more sentences on the back of this worksheet.

Sports

1. **What is missing?** Complete the picture below.
2. **What is the situation?** Give the picture a title.

....

3. **What can you see in the picture?** Write down words.

to do a handstand – to play – shorts –

....

....

....

4. **What is happening?** Write your story on a piece of paper.

Give each person a name and say where they are.
Describe what everyone is doing.
Think about what will happen next.

Forest

Stories about sports & activities

Forest

1. **What is missing?** Complete the picture below.
2. **What is the situation?** Pick a title.
   - ☐ Camping in the forest
   - ☐ Exploring the forest
3. **What can you see in the picture?** Connect the words with the picture.

tree • sun • path • rubbish • hat • leaf • hut • to walk

bottle • to pick up • rucksack • fire • forest ranger • bag • to look • fox

4. **What is happening?** Complete the sentences.

In the fall, ...

A girl ....

Two kids ....

But suddenly, ...

Write 3–5 more sentences on the back of this worksheet.

Forest

1. **What is missing?** Complete the picture below.
2. **What is the situation?** Give the picture a title.

....

3. **What can you see in the picture?** Write down words.

tree – sunny – to pick up –

....

....

....

4. **What is happening?** Write your story on a piece of paper.

Give each person a name and say where they are.
Describe what everyone is doing.
Think about what will happen next.

Spring

Spring

1. **What is missing?** Complete the picture below.
2. **What is the situation?** Pick a title.
   - ☐ A day in the forest
   - ☐ A picnic in the park
3. **What can you see in the picture?** Connect the words with the picture.

bird • worm • to run • sun • cloud • to sit • grass • dog

bike • basket • baby • bottle • salad • butterfly • flower • dress • egg

4. **What is happening?** Complete the sentences.

On a sunny spring day, ...

On the blanket, there are ....

Suddenly, ...

One of the boys ....

Write 3–5 more sentences on the back of this worksheet.

Spring

1. **What is missing?** Complete the picture below.
2. **What is the situation?** Give the picture a title.

....

3. **What can you see in the picture?** Write down words.

bicycles – to run – happy – ....

....

....

....

4. **What is happening?** Write your story on a piece of paper.

Give each person a name and say where they are.
Describe what everyone is doing.
Think about what will happen next.

Summer

Seasonal stories

Summer

1. **What is missing?** Complete the picture below.
2. **What is the situation?** Pick a title.
   ☐ Holidays by the sea
   ☐ Holidays in the mountains
3. **What can you see in the picture?** Connect the words with the picture.

sun • sand • umbrella • couple • beach • sunglasses • ice cream • hotel

boat • to swim • to read • sun hat • water • book • wave • shorts

4. **What is happening?** Complete the sentences.

In the summer holidays, ...

There are ....

The girl ....

In the sea, ...

Write 3–5 more sentences on the back of this worksheet.

Summer

1. **What is missing?** Complete the picture below.
2. **What is the situation?** Give the picture a title.

....

3. **What can you see in the picture?** Write down words.

to swim – sunglasses – ice cream – ....

....

....

....

4. **What is happening?** Write your story on a piece of paper.

Give each person a name and say where they are.
Describe what everyone is doing.
Think about what will happen next.

Autumn

Autumn

1. **What is missing?** Complete the picture below.
2. **What is the situation?** Pick a title.
   - ☐ A windy afternoon in autumn
   - ☐ A sunny day in the city
3. **What can you see in the picture?** Connect the words with the picture.

   house • tree • wind • costume • street • sunflower • to play • leaves

   pumpkin • witch • window • scarf • lantern • animals • bush • jacket

4. **What is happening?** Complete the sentences.

   On a stormy day, ...

   Three children are wearing costumes and .... ,

   but ....

   Suddenly, ...

Write 3–5 more sentences on the back of this worksheet.

Autumn

1. **What is missing?** Complete the picture below.
2. **What is the situation?** Give the picture a title.

....

3. **What can you see in the picture?** Write down words.

lantern – to play – scarf – ....

....

....

....

4. **What is happening?** Write your story on a piece of paper.

Give each person a name and say where they are.
Describe what everyone is doing.
Think about what will happen next.

Winter

Winter

1. **What is missing?** Complete the picture below.
2. **What is the situation?** Pick a title.
   - ☐ Fun on the beach
   - ☐ Fun in the snow
3. **What can you see in the picture?** Connect the words with the picture.

house • to build • star • snowball fight • scarf • snow • sledge • lake

snowman • to fall • hat • to walk • to skate • ice • ice skates

4. **What is happening?** Complete the sentences.

On a cold winter day ....

Some kids ....

Other people ....

Suddenly, a man ....

Write 3–5 more sentences on the back of this worksheet.

Winter

1. **What is missing?** Complete the picture below.
2. **What is the situation?** Give the picture a title.

....

3. **What can you see in the picture?** Write down words.

lake – to skate – snowman – ....

....

....

....

4. **What is happening?** Write your story on a piece of paper.

Give each person a name and say where they are.
Describe what everyone is doing.
Think about what will happen next.

Ghosts

Ghosts

1. **What is missing?** Complete the picture below.
2. **What is the situation?** Pick a title.
   - ☐ A visit to the castle at midnight
   - ☐ A visit to the castle in the afternoon
3. **What can you see in the picture?** Connect the words with the picture.

castle • flag • bat • moon • star • tower • bush

sign • window • ghost • door • to open • bike • to be frightened • tyre

4. **What is happening?** Complete the sentences.

In the middle of the night, ...

In the castle, they ....

The girl ....

The boy ....

Write 3–5 more sentences on the back of this worksheet.

Ghosts

1. **What is missing?** Complete the picture below.
2. **What is the situation?** Give the picture a title.

....

3. **What can you see in the picture?** Write down words.

   castle – frightened – to open –

   ....

   ....

   ....

   ....

4. **What is happening?** Write your story on a piece of paper.

Give each person a name and say where they are.
Describe what everyone is doing.
Think about what will happen next.

Superheroes

Fantastical stories

Superheroes

1. **What is missing?** Complete the picture below.
2. **What is the situation?** Pick a title.
   - ☐ The superheroes stop the bank robbers
   - ☐ The superheroes are having a sandwich
3. **What can you see in the picture?** Connect the words with the picture.

   to break in • house • door • mask • moon • to laugh • costume • star

glass • window • tattoo • bank robber • boots • skirt • belt • bush

4. **What is happening?** Complete the sentences.

   In the middle of the night, ...,

   but ....

   The bank robbers ....

   The superheroes ....

Write 3–5 more sentences on the back of this worksheet.

Superheroes

1. **What is missing?** Complete the picture below.
2. **What is the situation?** Give the picture a title.

....

3. **What can you see in the picture?** Write down words.

bank robbers – to break in – mask – ....

....

....

....

4. **What is happening?** Write your story on a piece of paper.

Give each person a name and say where they are.
Describe what everyone is doing.
Think about what will happen next.

Robot

Robot

1. **What is missing?** Complete the picture below.
2. **What is the situation?** Pick a title.
   - ☐ A robot for doing my homework
   - ☐ A robot for washing the dishes
3. **What can you see in the picture?** Connect the words with the picture.

antenna • robot • book • desk • exercise book • pencil • t-shirt

tools • to do homework • to invent • to smile • trousers • to sit

4. **What is happening?** Complete the sentences.

On Friday afternoon, ...

She ....

So, she ....

The robot ....

Write 3–5 more sentences on the back of this worksheet.

Robot

1. **What is missing?** Complete the picture below.
2. **What is the situation?** Give the picture a title.

....

3. **What can you see in the picture?** Write down words.

to invent – homework – proud – ....

....

....

....

4. **What is happening?** Write your story on a piece of paper.

Give each person a name and say where they are.
Describe what everyone is doing.
Think about what will happen next.

Hilfekarten

Vor dem Schreiben: Das Bild beschreiben

Bevor du anfängst, deine Geschichte zu schreiben, beschreibe das Bild einem Partner oder einer Partnerin. Beschreibe den Ort, die Personen und ihre Aktivitäten.

Diese Satzanfänge helfen dir dabei:

In the picture, I can see … The picture shows …
In the foreground, there is/are … In the background, there is/are … In the centre of the picture, there is/are …
On the left side of the picture … On the right side of the picture …
In front of …, there is/are … Next to …, there is/are … Behind …, there is/are …

Vor dem Schreiben: Schreibideen finden

Schreibe und male viele kleine Schreibideen auf ein Blatt.
Deine Schreibideen sollten lustig, spannend, gruselig, interessant, überraschend … sein.

bank robbers run away

…

ideas

…

stop the bank robbers

use their superpowers

Hilfekarten

Vor dem Schreiben: W-Fragen beantworten

Deine Geschichte sollte die W-Fragen beantworten:
Wann? Wo? Wer? Was? Wie? Warum?
Mache dir vor dem Schreiben Notizen zum Ort, zur Zeit usw.

Diese Wörter helfen dir dabei:

When?	this morning, on Monday afternoon, in the winter, yesterday …
Where?	in the park/forest, at home, at the beach/pool, in the city, by the lake …
Who?	children, a family, a girl, a boy, a group of friends …
What?	a picnic, a party, a holiday, writing a letter, tidying up …
How?	quickly, slowly, loudly, quietly, carefully, in a friendly way …
Why?	because …

Beim Schreiben: Gute Geschichten erzählen

Erzähle eine lustige oder spannende Geschichte, indem du etwas Überraschendes oder Unerwartetes passieren lässt. Schiebe Gespräche, Fragen, Gedanken und Gefühle ein.

Diese Satzanfänge helfen dir dabei:

conversations	He/she says/said: "…", He/she shouts/shouted: "…" He/she asks/asked: "…", He/she answers/answered: "…"
questions	Who …? When …? Where …? What …? How …? Why …? Do you …? Does he/she …? Did you …? Did he/she …?
thoughts	He/she thinks/thought: "…"
feelings	They feel happy, sad, tired, bored, excited, worried, angry, frightened …

Hilfekarten

Beim Schreiben: Zeitangaben machen

Schreibe deine Geschichte in der richtigen Reihenfolge auf.
Alle müssen deine Geschichte verstehen können.

Diese Wörter helfen dir dabei:

First, … Then, … Next, … Later, … In the end, … Finally, …
In the morning, … At noon, … In the afternoon, … In the evening, … At night, … At 3 o'clock … On the next day, …

Beim Schreiben: Sinneseindrücke beschreiben

Beschreibe, was die Personen in deiner Geschichte sehen, riechen, fühlen, hören oder schmecken.

Diese Wörter helfen dir dabei:

to see	a ghost, his/her/their friends, trees in the forest, the cake …
to smell	the fresh air, flowers, the food, something burning …
to feel	the soft grass, the hard floor, the icy snow, the hot sand, the cold water …
to hear	a loud noise, a strange sound, a scream, someone laughing …
to taste	the delicious ice cream, a piece of cake …

Hilfekarten

Beim Schreiben: Beschreiben, wie etwas ist

Beschreibe die Dinge, Orte und Personen genauer.

Diese Wörter helfen dir dabei:

number	one, two, three, four, five, six, seven, eight, nine, ten, eleven, twelve, many, a lot of, a few ...
opinion	good, bad, great, terrible, fantastic, lovely, silly, frightening, lazy, beautiful, pretty, ugly, strange, wonderful, funny, interesting, boring, brilliant ...
mood	happy, sad, angry, hungry, rude, adventurous, brave, excited, friendly, bored, surprised, annoyed ...
size	small, big, tall, little, gigantic, tiny, long, short ...
colours	white, black, yellow, blue, red, green, violet, pink, brown, orange, grey ...

Beim Schreiben: Ein Ende schreiben

Überlege dir,

- ob deine Geschichte positiv oder negativ endet.
- was die Personen am Ende machen.
- wie die Personen sich am Ende fühlen.
- ob das Problem gelöst wird.

Diese Sätze helfen dir dabei:

In the end, ...
What a great day it had been!
They lived happily ever after.
And so, the big adventure ended.
The end.

Hilfekarten

Nach dem Schreiben: Den Text kontrollieren

Achte auf die Groß- und Kleinschreibung. Diese Wörter schreibt man im Englischen groß:

➯ Satzanfänge (z. B.: **In** the morning, she goes to school by bus.)
➯ Namen von Menschen oder Orten (z. B.: **M**ary, **M**r Patil, **C**hicago)
➯ das Pronomen „I" (z. B.: In the summer, **I** go to the beach.)
➯ Monate, Tage, Feiertage (z. B. His birthday is in **A**ugust. It is **C**hristmas.)

Kontrolliere die Zeiten.

➯ Wenn deine Geschichte in der Gegenwart spielt, nutzt du simple present oder present progressive.
z. B. Laura **goes** to school at 9 o'clock in the morning. The sun **is shining**.

➯ Wenn deine Geschichte in der Vergangenheit spielt, nutzt du simple past oder past progressive.
z. B. Laura **went** to school in the morning. The sun **was shining**.

Ist alles richtig geschrieben? Schlage schwierige Wörter im Wörterbuch nach.

Nach dem Schreiben: Die Geschichte verbessern

Lies deine Geschichte einem Partner oder einer Partnerin vor. Stelle ihm oder ihr dann die folgenden Fragen und notiere seine oder ihre Einschätzung.

	☺	😐	☹
Did you understand everything?			
Does the story match the picture?			
Is something missing?			
Does the story have a good heading?			
Is the story interesting?			
Does the story have a matching ending?			

Selbsteinschätzung

Aufgabe: Kreuze an, wie gut dir die folgenden Dinge gelungen sind.

	☺	😐	☹
Ich habe vor dem Schreiben passende Wörter notiert.			
Ich habe vor dem Schreiben Ideen zur Handlung gesammelt.			
Meine Geschichte hat eine passende Überschrift.			
Meine Geschichte beantwortet die W-Fragen.			
Meine Geschichte passt zum Bild.			
Meine Geschichte hat eine logische Reihenfolge.			
Meine Geschichte ist spannend.			
Meine Geschichte hat einen passenden Schluss.			
Ich habe verschiedene Satzanfänge benutzt.			
Ich habe meine Geschichte auf Fehler überprüft.			
Mein Partner/meine Partnerin konnte meiner Geschichte folgen.			

Ich fand meine Geschichte ....,

weil ....

....

....

Diese Wörter habe ich neu gelernt: ....

....

....

Beim nächsten Mal ....

....

....